DORIS KLEIN

Poems and Paintings by
"The Radio Poet"

LONGMEADOW PRESS

For my darling husband, Leon

The following poems have appeared in the Metropolitan Diary
feature of the *New York Times:* "Retribution" (as "To Number
Two Son"), "View," "After February," "Courtyard," "Summer
Tenement," "Nightcaps," "What Is So Rare," "First Snow,"
"Gingko," "Yellow Weather."

"The Insect" first appeared in the Home Forum of *The Christian
Science Monitor.*

Cover design by Dorothy Wachtenheim

Interior design by Richard Oriolo

Library of Congress Cataloging-in-Publication Data

Klein, Doris, 1916–
    Doris Klein : poems and paintings / by the "Radio Poet." — 1st
ed.
        p.   cm.
    ISBN: 0-681-00784-2
    I. Title.   II. Title: Poems and paintings.
PS6561.L3444D67   1995
811'.54 — dc20   94-38917
                                                        CIP

Printed in Singapore

First Edition

0 9 8 7 6 5 4 3 2 1

CONTENTS

INTRODUCTION   5

WHAT COLOR IS ALONE?

The New Studio After Your Death   7
To Maryia   8
Twin Beds   9
Traveler   11
Noon   12
Nightmare   13
You Will Never Hear My Poem   14
What Color Is White?   15
Tenant   17

TALCUM POWDER SKY

Nightcaps   19
After February   19
Suddenly   20
Gingko   22
Poem for Purple Tulips   23
Yellow Weather   24
Summer Tenement   26
Evening Magic   26
View   27
Rooftop   28
What Is So Rare   28
Summer Locker   29
Changes   30
First Snow   31
After Snow   31
Courtyard   33

CHILDREN IN CONFETTI

Snapshots   35
Retribution   36
The Snapshot Posing at Eight Years Old   37
Incubator: Hospital Window   39
The Kite at Montauk   40

IN A BLUE DREAMED-OF PLACE

Painting   42
The Black Wave (To Georgia O'Keeffe)   43
Today   44
Love Affair   45
Nightmare Still Life   46
The Bridge at Arles   48
The Impressionists' Party   48
Exhibit — Francis Bacon   49
The Sixth   50

THE SIGNATURE OF BIRDS

Feathers   52
Bee   53
The Insect   54
Two Haiku   55
The Chipmunk   56
To a Tabby   57

LANDSCAPE OF RENEWAL

Raggedy Ann   59
Voyager   60
The Vase   62
Post-operative   63
Saga of the Shoes   64

INTRODUCTION

It would be too easy, and too simplistic, to say that I discovered Doris Klein. In truth, Doris discovered WABC talk radio and what a good thing that was.

Talk radio is the only real town meeting left in America. The phone lines are open and the opinions and ideas flow in like a swift-moving river. No topic is too serious or too silly for talk radio: my audience has contemplated whether it would be better to be able to fly or to be invisible; we have debated the right to be gay in the military and have discussed health care, gun control and the merits and demerits of nearly every national and local political candidate who has emerged during the fifteen years that I have been a radio talk show host. I have interviewed senators, actors, actresses and authors of both fiction and nonfiction. Though my business is talk, I've sometimes played music and interviewed musicians.

There is plenty of talk on talk radio, from the substantive to the silly, but there is one thing almost never heard — POETRY. That is, until one Saturday morning in the summer of 1993 when "Doris from Manhattan" (it was months before we even discovered her last name) called in and read her first poem for the WABC audience.

Her calls became a weekly event. We always chatted a bit, but the shining jewel of each call was the poem of the week. Doris's poems covered, a wide range of human experience, from nature and children to golf and painting; from the joy of love to the pain of loss. And so, at least on my show, the level of talk radio rises a bit each week with the addition of a new element — dare I say it? — ART.

So I won't take credit for discovering Doris Klein. But I am certainly glad Doris discovered WABC and gave me the opportunity to be the conduit that will allow her poetry and her art to reach the large and appreciative audience it deserves.

LYNN SAMUELS
WABC Radio
New York, New York

WHAT COLOR
IS ALONE?

The New Studio After Your Death

You moved me here
and left before unpacking.
Fragments of yesterday
lie in unopened cartons.
Canvases lean wearily against strange walls.
Shopping bags slouch,
heavy with their plastic pregnancies
of drawings.

I move slowly,
as from an old illness.
Wondering where my colors are,
or the "wonder glue" that
collaged things together.

What color is alone?
It is here . . .
It inhabits my clothing,
purples my scarves,
sifts from my sleeves.

This new place has a light at early morning,
A jonquil light; a yellowness . . .
Why do I find it beige?

Dearest,

Where did you put my palette?

To Maryia

He is gone, I said,
my light is gone
there is no light.

She looked at me,
eyes filling like blue wings,
just looked at me.

And in her looking,
there was this touch, so vast,
I can't explain it.

And grasses rose up and bent,
grasses against grasses,
in the meadow of her eyes.

Need is such a lonesome wound.
Words, usually flowing,
press themselves flat against the teeth,
the tongue catches on its hinges
with crazy lockings.

We leaned
as grasses lean,
one against the other.

The wild blue of her eyes
reaching,
reaching my pain.

Twin Beds

Last night you called my name and I awoke.
Pummeled from the dark
tunnel of sleep, I listen
again for your voice; how you
said my name,
clear as air
across beds we shared.

My packages lie on your spread.
Bandages from Bloomingdale's.
The lacy slip, patent leather shoes,
a bra to knock 'em dead,
slit down to there.

The children sleep undisturbed.
They do not hear that
night alarm.
Only I,
in the darkest pit of
where I hide
can hear your voice, your call,
or,
am I dreaming still.

Traveler

Against the corner of your mouth
a thread of rust. A spittle.
I hear the thin rattle of breath,
or is there breath?
I force a tunnel between my
lips and yours.
"Do not go," I say.
But you were on a journey I could not follow.

At first I only noticed his abandoned shoes.
The air was chill, typical of November
and the chance of snow.
Strangers lock themselves as gates.
Medics work hard.
I hear a chest bone break,
the heavy thwack; the in and out of breath,
or, is there breath?

You traveled light that night.
Nothing of weight remains.
I am keeper of small holdings,
where light plays shy with grass.
I touch your still life,
the place where your pillow sleeps.
You are home.

The subway steps are granite gray and tall.
I walk them
slowly. . . .

Noon

Juggling packages from the A&P,
fumbling with keys, slowly I
ease myself
into the long hall.
Light places a scrim across the day
as though shy
at being seen.

Noon. The hour stands on tip-toe
pressing the hands of the
clock into forever.

I think stew. I always think stew in winter
as though it were a poultice.
Onions snuggling against carrots,
a soupçon of wine.
I'd say "Beef Bourguignonne,"
and you would always say "stew."

I pause beside the kitchen door,
contemplate the evening's meal,
feel
the loneliness of
ham and eggs.

Nightmare

Then comes the hour between three and four,
when car signals send Motherwells to
bedroom beams,
scenes I know by heart,
where lights collide
but never provide sleep.

Between five and six,
a quasi-peace enters my arms.
My hands cross my belly
and I breathe deep into
night's dark embryo.

A dream of loss repeats:

You've just come through an open door.
"I'm cold," you say.
I press myself against your gray shape
to burn you into being.
You are not there.

My body sweat turns sheets into mummy gowns.
The Bosch carousel winds down.
I lean from my black and blue bed
and reach for morning;
the toothbrush,
the hope of
orange juice.

You Will Never Hear My Poem

You will never hear my poem;
it is performed
on a stage of white desolation.
I am Bip
slow-motioned
against the endless wind,
my braille touch
searching the boarded planes
of your ears.
I am Petrushka
helpless in cotton,
battling against the
stone
of your deafness.
Against shut windows,
closed piano's
empty rooms,
you will never hear my poem.
I am old fruit,
my flesh withering
against the skin
eating silence.

What Color Is White?

It is alone.
It is a cry that echoes.
It is uninhabited.
It is skimmed milk
on a table set for caviar.
It is linen without pattern,
clay without sculpture,
It is death.

I have lived long with white since
you have gone.
No color succors me.
You were my feast.

I sleep,
huddled against my bones.
The awful white;
my bed,
my pillow,
my gown.

Tenant

You have taken up residence
in the alcove of my mind.
A troubled tenant.

February. The air congeals.
Ceilings sprout veins; drip
onto wallpaper.
The glue unsizes
leaving a curl of damp roses.
In the kitchen,
the sink drools
a foliage of rust.

From this bed where I dream you,
rain splatters the sill,
fills the room where there
are no seams.
I stare at moldings, roofbeams,
remain weightless under gray sheets.
You lurk
above the covers of my mind.

When dark breaks,
I hear you walk
in the attic of my mind.
Confined to space where there is no exit,
no eviction.

TALCUM POWDER SKY

Nightcaps

The sudden taste of white!
A talcum powder sky
sends icy visitors
to hold the city in
fragile imprisonment.

Traffic slows, lights
blur in ghost-gray air.
My cat curls as Buddha near my bed.

On the street,
the lampposts wear white nightcaps . . . .

After February

When winter winds
prevail
and rain comes down
to soak us,
And all our dreamings
fail,
And life slips out
of focus.
What I would give
to have
The chutzpah of
the crocus!

Suddenly

The winds of March are here.
Half winter now, but
far beneath the earth
a sleeping April.
Thoughts of seasons wing
from every bird that
solicits on Fifth Avenue.
Bonnets nod on Afro hairdos.
Roses take over a window
at Bloomingdale's.

My kid climbs high on his
Daddy's shoulder and
crows like a king . . .

It's Spring!

Gingko

Skipping along
careless as a
potsy
allowing your frilled skirt
to be splashed
by rain.
Coquette
flirting with water;
you're an artiful dodger
teasing
manholes.
Hard for me to
follow
small
fan on the pavement,
spilling
yellow.

Poem For Purple Tulips

They arabesque, topless in their vase.
Leaves snake without modesty,
not too shy
to belly dance the air!

Tulips, oh tulips,
time has turned
all that mauve to silver.
Your shapes begin to quiver,
to fall . . .

Purples turn
to black.

My garbage pail
tonight,
wears mourning . . .

Yellow Weather

Plying the wind,
the grass stretches itself into yellow.
Forsythia unwinds yards of topaz
spilling sunlight onto highways.
Dandelions sew buttons on lawns; a field
of jonquils, cupping gold,
hems a meadow.

This is Apriltide.
I gather sprays of
shy mimosa, place them
in the Art Deco vase,
watch them as they churn,
the light pouring from
them in a fever
of yellow.

Summer Tenement

Windows yawn,
curtains stretch past the bravery
of geraniums to reach early morning sun.
The Hopper girl, in pink curlers,
looks in a mirror,
applies mascara.
An orange cat curls
against the crooked slats of home.

Wash lines drool socks.
Jeans boast Clorox mistakes against gray bricks.
Cut glass windows reflect
purple skies,
russet sunsets,
like
wish you were here
postcards.

Evening Magic

It is sunset.
The nightly magician appears,
drops his crimson and orange ball,
onto the horizon;
a perfect lobshot to ace the sky!
On the Jersey shore miniature fireworks
find see-through windows and
drop from floor to floor,
like a child's sparkler playing peekaboo.
The old day departs.
I wear another summer in my heart.

View

Windows flame
to diamond; clouds
puff,
their capes are
gray drift.
The sky turns September.
The sluggish Hudson
tugs its pewter;
barges pull into evening.
Firefly skylights blink
in Morse code
calling night to dinner.

Summer leans on
my sill.
A window box across the street
sends flowers . . .

Rooftop

A girl in a bikini
leans over the roof of a brownstone,
watches the street.
Boys with beer cans
place blankets near a skylight.
They anoint themselves with oil.
In the warm colors of a May morning,
Tar Beach opens!

It is that time of year again.
Iced tea time,
You and me time.
Freckles . . .
The satisfying itch of sunburn.

What Is So Rare

Summer stretches like a rubber band.
Ice-cream-cone days,
your hand in
my hand.
Wink of a plaid tie,
sigh of a summer dress.
We walk in candy-colored air,
our footsteps
a conspiracy.
Hand in hand,
the long way home.

Summer Locker

Cleaned out
stretch pants
ice-cream shirts
jeans
put aside
clubs
I'd made excuses for
Lip-liners
eyelashes
cards, stashed in
upside down
dizziness
cleats
needing shoes
plastic shower caps
the Pucci suit,
I never swam laps in.
harlequin glasses that
winked at
the last party.

Retain
at best
the empty flask,
the plumage dress
reminiscent of
the peacock
season.

Need the russet change,
winter scratch
of thermal underwear.

Changes

I swallow sky,
gorge like a drunk on cranberry and wine.
Thirst on pools where geese turn
feathered cartwheels,
splashing joy.

Another season ends.
A small tree unties her green dress;
changes into a golden apron.
Apricot and flame
crunch like Wheaties; my
heels burst confetti!

Spun-sugar clouds scud
against blue.
Wind rises, welcoming the
evening's darkness.

I raise my eyes,
wonder about the new year changes.
Autumn,
a tough act to follow.

First Snow

Quiet as cotton
softer than a secret,
a talcum sky
sends down messengers.
A chorus line of white
taps at my cheek,
kicks at my heels.
I stick out my tongue
to savor the cold taste
of winter's icy flavor.

After Snow

A winter storm slips out to sea.
Pigeons "rudder down,"
hit the ice
like feathered skiers.
Gargoyles on buildings
wear white shawls.
Ghost clouds puff from brownstone chimneys.
Cranky shovels screech and scrape
to make sidewalks clear,
and children in confetti snowsuits,
shout laughter in the snow white air!

Courtyard

Snow has a way of just coming down.
It whitens the mind.
The courtyard sets up her bazaar with
an eye for drama.
The dilemma of the unmatched shoe.
The kinky track of hairpins.
The missing B from the Scrabble game:
Scattered postcards
from Miami.
All
attempt a grace; assume something
they cannot be,
as though each item knew
snow
would make it special
now.

CHILDREN IN
CONFETTI

Snapshots

Child,
your Fourth of July body explodes.
The playground slide
rockets you
into your Mother's arms.

In the field,
a Roman candle of red tulips
licks your waist.

High on the swing,
you dazzle the sky.
Small sparkler,
full of second-year speed,
nothing holds the booming sound of
your joy.

Small child.
You pinwheel my mind.

Retribution

I was a bad child,
that I know.
Didn't obey,
didn't eat slow.
Slammed the doors
ran the street,
walked the house
in stockinged feet.
Grew too big,
much too tall.
Couldn't remember
prayers at all.
Hated homework,
loathed my bed,
"Caused gray hairs"
my Mother said.

But now I'm grown
and is it fair
to pay for sins
from way back there?

But if it's fair
then I can see
why this small child
belongs to me!

The Snapshot
Posing at Eight Years Old

She was all grace;
I was awkward grass.
Summer bloomed us together
on one hundred and fiftieth street.
Idolatry began
the day she asked me
to play.

My Daddy held his camera.
I saw her hold out her skirt to curtsy,
preening for the camera buff.
My Dad said:
"Hon, let's snap the two of you,"
and mincing shy,
with skirt held out,
I "cheesed" it too.

Maxine,
I never will forget,
standing in her shadow,
wanting with every breath of me
to be Maxine,
as beautiful as she!

I hold that snapshot now,
remembering that passion wish,
so deep
so shattering.
"To be Maxine!"
as beautiful as she!

Incubator: Hospital Window

Last night, through glass,
I watched the universe.
A shape, small as a leaf
twines aginst the pillow of his Mother.
With one finger,
she travels the silken
glade of his cheek,

Rocks to his sucking,
her hair in tendrils of abstraction,
eyes filling: holding
a lullaby in Pampers.

Outside the window,
I imagine his breath,
trembling
as wet fern . . .

The Kite at Montauk

After small proddings
I seem to rise with you.
You pull yourself free,
find wind currents
and slalom wild against scudding clouds,
turning and twisting
with a life of your own.

Winds gain speed; my arms
lend direction,
knowing that sooner or later
I will have to guide you back.
How heavy you became!
There was this curious feeling
to let you go; not strain so hard
for your return.
But,
were you not mine?

Bright plastic being,
you fought coming home
till the last.
Then dipped,
flopped,
came to rest up-ended on the dunes.

My poor Petrushka . . .

I lift you sadly,
bring you back to the beach house.
Confused, that a toy with string
would make me want to apologize.

IN A BLUE
DREAMED-OF PLACE

Painting

She lies in a blue dreamed-of place,
complacent, as though
the frenzy of hands
had never put her there.

An acorn hat, with the
blue-checked headband,
peers through the
long dune grass.

Serenity stretches the
placid flesh of her hands
as they drift on a
soft denim skirt.

Supine on the
clay-cool of sand, she rests.
Sun lightens the silken
sheen of her hair.

Grasses spiral towards the
white of her blouse.
White as a saints white
and cool, as I have never been

Nor could be . . .

The Black Wave
(To Georgia O'Keeffe)

Over the hard wet beach
the lighthouse burns.
A star in the gray
of evening light.
The horizontal light
precedes the wave,
spills its silken ruffle
on venetian sand.
Cinnabar greens lapse
into indigos,
turn timid,
collapse on land
as waves do at dusk.

Dawn at six
plays tricks with oranges and pinks;
plucks at waves,
soap-bubbling them to shore.
They spill, splash,
lash at bare toes
seeking wet autographs.

Evening brings rain
in vertical grooves,
siphoning color from landscape
with the indifference of gray sieves.
Sends me in shivers towards

the warmth of
dry house slippers.

My painting leans her
linen face against the wall.

Weary as a hammock,
I blot out seascape with drawn shades,
as still another evening huddles down . . .

Today

I saw Clara in the supermarket,
a great Artist years ago.

Hands like antlers
grip the shopping cart.

"God sakes, a loaf of bread
a dollar fifty?" she whines.

Wonder about surviving
but on coming closer

observe her eyeshadow
an astonishing shade of blue!

Love Affair

You walked into my landscape
and made revisions.

Dark cypresses were turned to catch
the sun's face,
meadows, going nowhere,
you stained with roadways
of return.

Pouring oil on my
matte turpentine,
you gave glow to opaque shadows.

Feeding flowers to a vase of
delft blue,
you changed my
still life.

Why are we perfect together?

I am adjustable.

Nightmare Still Life

The basket was diapered in black wool.
On one side
an ice-green sandal
slunk like a whore
against
the *New York Times*.

Stiffly erect, a paintbrush,
like a huge bubble pipe,
birthed an egg!

The Coney Island pencil
was "making it" with the
casaba melon,
completely ignoring a
pear,
which lay fast asleep
against knit two, purl two.

"Who put the sculptured Queen Anne's lace there?" I said.
"It's ugly; its face pocked."

Then the basket was passed around
pretentiously
and all the people
oohed and aahed and
compared it to Cezanne.

The Bridge at Arles

He painted it yellow and with
pale blue strokes,
washed in a distant sky.
I imagine myself there, near
where the lime-green grasses
jut from the river bank and the
cream sand lies still against sheer water.
I dream his palette, hungry with color,
eager to catch the elusive spark
of light before it slips beneath clouds,
crosses the bridge and
dips into dark . . .

The Impressionists' Party

Manet suggested we
party in the garden.
Pissarro brought wine and
invited Cezanne, who
treated to oranges.

Renoir brought children, all
apple-cheeked and rosy,
Monet made haystacks, we
all had a ball! Gauguin
brought brown-skinned girls most
colorful in muu muus
and Degas made ballet dancers
out of us all!

Exhibit — Francis Bacon

I enter the arena
where paintings roar from
glassed-in cages —
Ropes of color spill
like bleeding meat.

Bowel-hunched figures
press against dark shapes,
vomit a
monologue of grief.

Wounds open,
bubble into screams from
tortured portraits

as Voyeur,
a single light
peers
into mattresses
through cubicles
of flesh,
down,
through groin, groan
to the ultimate cold of
bone.

"In the end"
he said,
"it is called despair."

Believing this,
I walk quickly
to exit one, and
keep walking.

The Sixth

I am ill from you.
Your tentative starts,
like fetal turnings,
bring on listlessness.
Drowsy as a pillow,
I resist decisions; a
stranger to my own hand.
Colors take on past tense,
bleed off,
like lost leaves.

Yet today,
you assume perspective.
I catch a glimpse of
sea and space,
trace
the still heart of
your laden table.
You have become a bright pink field
of orange and gold silk,
where apples tease against
pale china cups.

I sign a new painting.

THE SIGNATURE
OF BIRDS

Feathers

Gentle warrior, I hold your plumage.
Salvaged from old golf caps
and summer grasses.
The goose feather that tickled the wind
that Indian summer.
The black quill of the crow
when snow fell
and apples lay underfoot.

Gray, undistinguished,
the pigeon's feather drifts on my sill.
I ring silver bells
and feed the sky!
These also
are your talismans.

I question the signature of birds; the
fragile feedback that
a sigh can blow away.
Still, this is all I have.
Or,
are you telling me with feathers
to be brave?

Bee

His timing was all wrong.
Never should have
buzzed around at
noon,
the room
so overcrowded.

And such commotion! Calling attention
to his size, shape,
the special down
of his jacket.

That awful swat,
reducing his golden sound
to mimosa
on the sill.

Had afterthoughts about that kill.
Haunted by what
he might have gleaned
from daffodil and tulip,
horny, with his velvet pouch of summer.

Feel a bummer.

Know now,
should have left that bee
be.

The Insect

Rescued,
gingerly
rinsed with water
he lies on Kleenex,
a
small Rorschach blob.
I take him to the window,
an August sun providing
fans for his revival.

Fingernail
against his innards,
I lift him into some kind
of action.
He whirrs for a second,
then stops.

Has he lost an antenna?
A foot perhaps?
I search in vain,
ask how many feet he should have
in the first place.
The Art-Deco wings
intricate but fragile
seemed secure.
So nudge him into flight,
place him on the window,
where he suddenly
gums up on his own!

Is he ready?

I believe so:
later,
coming back,
he is gone.

Small visitor,
send my greetings to the sky.

Two Haiku

I lifted her then,
the red thread of her song gone.
A small finch is dead.

Seashell in my hand
is now uninhabited.
This house is for sale.

The Chipmunk

A small form,
fragile in fur,
not meant to be a traveler in trees
but to your hand
extended on the grass.
A small death
that no one heard except yourself
who held his tender weight.
I guess we should not get
so unstrung
about a chipmunk,
but he was young.

To a Tabby

Come,
nest with me.
Your slow purr,
a drum of consolation.
Your silence,
a candle
in the dark place where I mourn.

Come,
fur beside me.
The warmth of your folding,
the tweed thirst
of your tongue,
a bandage for wounds.

Curl,
nudge once again.
Here where my arms need resting,
where pain
seeks a pillow . . .

LANDSCAPE
OF RENEWAL

Raggedy Ann

He turned my head to face a
pale green wall,
plucked at stitches on my chest
that once contained a pillow.
Pillow for the searching hand,
pillow for a cheek that nuzzled.
A baby's "nightcap" corner.
The yeasty pride of lilac sweaters . . .

I am Raggedy Ann.
Head turned to face
a pale green wall.
Beneath my stitchery,
no candy heart
beats consolation.

Voyager

There is always the wound
where the knife screeched.
Always,
a knowledge of theft.
I cry for the Miss America in me,
the loss
underneath the lilac sweater.

I lie on your bed,
an uncharted map.
In the language of mutes,
we voyage each other's scars; engravings
of smaller deaths.

Convalescents,
we touch,
asking only the touching back.
Patient beginners at an age-old game,
we have reached, late in our time,
a landscape of renewal.

The Vase

We bought it together last Christmas.
An ellipse of white bisque
with painted fronds and
gold stippling; orange flowers that
folded into lavender,
tendrils that moved upwards from the base,
forming a place
for the artist's signature.

"It is one of a kind," the
salesman said.

How to describe
the sudden breaking,
the beauty
no longer here?

Glue pieced it together,
but inside of me
lies its
irreparable crack.

Post-operative

We will talk about bones later.
They have a way of knitting together neatly.
Knit one. Purl two.
You never see them showing off.
Scars have no secrets.

My body seems a geography map.
Cross-hatched lines beginning here,
ending there . . .
Hem-stitched hills that reach
a plateau; slope off towards an indifferent moss.
The surgeon's artistry unsigned.
I am anonymous.

Still, were you to touch what is here
that has not been carved away,
a bird might envy my flight!
His wings would not chafe against the air,
but soar,

and death, a long way off.

Saga of the Shoes

I once owned a pair of sexy shoes.
Not just any pair,
but a go-to-hell, pointy-toed,
sling-backed,
wicked pair of shoes.
We waltzed at the Waldorf,
Rhumba'd at Roseland,
Slunk at Le Cirque . . .
Outliving their last, cast them in
the garbage, where a vendor
with flair grabbed the pair!
Down at the heels; trafficking
with the sleaze of all unwanted things,
hopeful that by chance,
some dame would tote them home,
slip them on,
capture one last dance.